Your

NO B.S.

Wedding Guide

Your

NO B.S.

Wedding Guide

Brian Starkman

gatekeeper press™

Columbus, Ohio

Your No B.S. Wedding Guide

Published by Gatekeeper Press
2167 Stringtown Rd, Suite 109
Columbus, OH 43123-2989
www.GatekeeperPress.com

The editorial work for this book is entirely the product of the author.
Gatekeeper Press did not participate in and is not responsible for any
aspect of these elements.

Library of Congress Control Number: 2021936935

ISBN (paperback): 9781662911415
eISBN: 9781662911422

To my Luv:

Thank you for being you and for always believing in me and my dreams. I love you!

To my twins:

Nothing gives me more joy than being your dad and watching you grow.

I love you Tay & Kay!

To my family:

Your continued love and support means the world to me!

And to the four very special people who helped me take my videography company to new heights, BH, DB, CH, CZ:

I am forever grateful for you!

Your No B.S. Wedding Guide

Table of Contents

Introduction: A Little B.S. (a.k.a. About Brian Starkman, Your Author)

Chapter 1: *Why* Have a Wedding?

Chapter 2: The Myth of Social Media (a.k.a. The Truth About What You See)

Chapter 3: Budget... How Much & How Do You Bankroll the Big Event?

Chapter 4: *Where* on Earth Do You Get Hitched?

Chapter 5: Do You Hire a Coordinator?

Chapter 6: Vendors, Vendors, Vendors

Chapter 7: Your Only Memories, Video & Pictures

Chapter 8: Everything Bridal Party

Chapter 9: *Who* Gets an Invitation?

Chapter 10: The First Look

Chapter 11: The Timeline (with samples)

Chapter 12: Crucial, No B.S. Tips That Don't Fit Anywhere Else

Chapter 13: What to Expect & My Hope for Your Big Day

Introduction

A Little B.S. (a.k.a. About *Brian Starkman*, Your Author)

Greetings! My name is Brian Starkman, and I am a veteran wedding videographer. Although your recent engagement may have led you to this guide, I am pretty sure that after you read it in its entirety, you're going to want to marry me (sorry folks, I'm taken).

My career in the wedding industry started in the 1990's, when I was about fifteen years old, well before I knew it would lead me down a 'forever path.' My, how time flies! I have had the pleasure of being a part of over one thousand events throughout those years, and I have gained endless amounts of experience.

I know you've got to be wondering (because I get the question a lot), "How did they trust you to film when you were so young?"

To start, that was not *exactly* the case.

See, I was always taught that hard work is the surest way to what you want. So, when it became time to drive and I desired the freedom that having a car offered, it was time to get to work.

It was amidst my high school job pursuit that I found myself walking through a beautiful courtyard called the French Quarter in the more suburban streets of Los Angeles. I was on my way to apply for a cashier position at a local Italian restaurant within the small complex. Some of my peers from school had luck getting a job there, and at the time, it seemed like an ideal place to work to me. However, life had much bigger plans for me in that moment, and I had no idea my life was about to change forever.

I was making my way along the brick path towards the restaurant's entrance, brainstorming how I'd answer certain interview questions if they were to arise. Suddenly, one of my close friend's dad's called out to me. He had been sitting outside of his office in the courtyard and noticed me walking up.

"Brian! What are you up to?" his question cut through the space loudly.

I remember our interaction like it was yesterday. How can I not in retrospect?

After filling him in on my goals of getting a job and a car, he simply said, "Why don't you come work for me?"

Of course, I asked what services he provided, and more importantly, what I would have to do. He told me he filmed events, and I would be scanning photos and creating montages for his videos. We both appreciated each other's straightforward approach, so I took the leap. And away our professional relationship went! Over the next several years, I was consistently given more responsibility and roles. I scanned photos, created montages, learned to edit, assisted filming select events, and even met and booked clients.

What's truly funny is that, thinking back to my teen years, weddings and love was not at the forefront of my mind. I mean, I was a typical teenage boy. I was focused more on things like school, girls, cars, and how loud I could get my car stereo to actually go. However, when I was present at my job, I always put my best foot forward. I was also sure to take in every bit of knowledge I could learn from my employers, as they had been in business a long time.

But the moment my perspective of videography switched will remain to be my most pivotal moment working at that first company. In fact, I could say it was truly what pushed me to see that my high school job had the potential to become *a career in the wedding industry*.

It was a day I had scheduled an in-studio meeting with a sweet, local couple who was extremely excited to be receiving their completed wedding video. See, back in the day ("when I was your age," haha), many couples came in to the studio to watch part of their video when it was done. I know, that seems almost impossible to imagine now! However, at that point it was a way for the videographer to show a portion of their work in good faith, and also to see the couple reap the benefit of their love story caught on camera.

When this particular couple came in, I could see the excitement etched on their faces.

They held hands as they watched their memories coming back to life right in front of them.

And while they did, I couldn't help but be struck by the tears streaming down the bride's cheeks, and the ones collecting in the groom's ducts, too. It was magical to watch happen, and also to know I helped facilitate that joy.

That was when the video light (or light bulb, in regular terms) flashed. This was my future, allowing couples and families beautiful glimpses of their most precious days. By that time it was 2005, and I was in my third year of college. I started thinking hard about my own company and how or when I would take the leap to create it. It seemed logical to wait until I graduated college, but sometimes what we plan doesn't always work out for one reason or another.

In fact, with perspective, I'd actually say it almost always seems to work out 'for better or worse.' Some problems were arising within the company I worked for, and on a hairpin move, I quickly decided I needed to start my own company. November 2005 arrived, I gave fair notice. By the time January 1, 2006 rolled around, my company was born.

I never looked back.

From there I went full force, booking as many events as possible and working almost every weekend. And for the record, I did complete all units and graduated college a short time later. It was quite an interesting, fun experience to go to a fraternity event one night and a wedding the next; talk about two opposite ends of the social spectrum.

Anyway, seven years after founding my company, *BGS Productions*, it was time for the wedding that mattered to me most... my own!

I applied all my years of knowledge to planning the most beautiful wedding I could to the most gorgeous woman I have ever met. She happily handed me the reins, too. In fact, she was pretty excited to attend one food tasting and then pass the torch to me. I had a blast planning a great event with our closest family and friends. And of course we had it filmed, which is something I will always be grateful for.

I had always known how important wedding videography was, but living the day of a client really put it in a different perspective. Especially because directly after our wedding, we were devastated by the loss of one of my best friends. A few years later my grandfather passed, followed shortly by my father-in-law. Despite our sadness, revisiting our own wedding video has re-infused us with so much love and endless live memories of these most special people.

In fact, amidst the process of writing this book, my wife and I were inspired to pull out our wedding video again.

Relatedly, we couldn't help but show our twins parts of it. To say they loved it would be an understatement. They kept calling out all the names of people they knew and had a blast dancing on our bed. It was incredibly touching to watch them sway along with many of the people we so dearly missed. Which only served to remind me of why I love my job even more.

Still, the most frequent question I get is, "But doesn't it get old going to weddings *every* weekend?"

And I realize the truest answer to that has become my reason for why I do what I do: I *love* LOVE! Amidst every event I capture I am constantly reminded why I love my field and what I do within it. There's nothing more exciting than capturing a part of someone's big day and allowing them to relive the "start" of their love story forever.

Also, I come from a bit of an 'older time.' A time when video equipment had huge costs and couldn't be shipped via the internet. Websites filled with vendor information and reviews had not been created yet. No one had a camera on their phone and social media was non-existent.

I know, imagine that!

However, I think by seeing the wedding industry go through all of these phases, I have been able to garner more knowledge and perspective than most. Maybe even more appreciation for it, while I'm at it.

That appreciation carries in to all of my initial meetings with my clients; they can see how much I love my work, which is always illustrated in my productions. Amidst these meetings, I have spent countless hours helping my clients by offering them advice about timelines, vendors, and so much more. As someone who treats everyone as a friend, it's important to me that I give my future and existing clients as much knowledge as possible without overwhelming them. That way each couple can make their most educated choices. And at the end of every meeting, I am always met with gratitude for the time and knowledge I share.

Which is *why* I wrote this book: to cut the excess during a rather hectic time and to pass along as much wedding wisdom as possible. I have truly seen it all (some of which I share in this book). In this guide I have taken the time to answer the most common wedding-planning questions and help you consider things that might happen along the way. I want to send you off with a soft start, and ease the planning process. So, let me be your guide, and *the only B.S. you deal with amidst the wedding process.* Hopefully you can rest assured and breathe easily even before your wedding is over. Remember, this should be a day full of joy, and the planning does not have to be any less.

-B.S.

Chapter 1

Why Have a Wedding?

Let's get straight to the point (I mean, that is why you're here, right?): *should you even have a wedding?*

I know, that's probably not the first question you imagined getting from a book helping you plan your big day. But my goal, as I said before, is to *keep it real.*

So, why even have a wedding? Well, let's consider a few things.

To start, why are you getting married in the first place? I mean, of course, you got engaged. A huge congratulations on the new beginning! No matter whether you just started marching down the aisle towards your future, or you have been engaged for some time, you've bought this book because you are considering hosting an event of variable size to celebrate your love. And that's exciting! After witnessing over twenty years of events, I still know in my heart that finding love is incredible. This makes me *so* happy for you, and also impels me to jump at the chance to help you plan.

But why a wedding? Why not just elope?

As tempting as that may sound, especially considering how difficult planning can be, I truly believe that every couple is deserving of an event fitting their own unique love story.

See, the way I have grown to view a wedding (again, based on attending thousands of them), the event isn't only to display the union of you and your spouse. It is a congregation and representation of all the things that make you a pair: your merging families and friends, your similar interests and loves, as well as the timeline of your tale. It is also (oftentimes) a once-in-a-lifetime celebration of all those things coming together at once and in one space.

I say this all the time, but you will most likely never have this same group of people celebrating in the same setting again.

This beautiful fragility of our wedding moments and memories was never more apparent than during my Wish Upon a Wedding experience. Philanthropy is both a professional and personal passion of mine, and one day I decided I wanted to marry them (pun intended). I browsed the internet for non-profits in the wedding industry and stumbled upon Wish Upon a Wedding, a foundation formed to help couples facing serious illness or life-altering circumstances plan their dream wedding. This non-profit brings together a venue and vendors who are willing to donate their services for free to ensure the couple receives an incredible wedding at *no cost*.

After reading about it, I had to sign up. I entered all my information on their site and within a few weeks, I was contacted to grant a wish to a wedding couple in San Diego, California (which is a relatively short two hour drive from me). I enthusiastically took the gig and met the couple not long after. We began by filming a bit about their love story, and I concluded the project with video of their wedding.

At their wedding, I met their family, friends and many new vendors I had never met before. The day was spectacularly smooth, which made it that much more special. I've had the chills aplenty at weddings before, but at this one they lasted the entire event. I could not keep thinking about how the bride had a life-changing illness, yet her expression showed no pain, nothing but pure joy.

When I delivered them their video, they absolutely flipped. It was clear to me that the experience bonded us forever. Unfortunately, the bride lost her battle against her illness and passed a few years after the wedding. And I know through this experience, that not only did I get to be a part of her most special day, but I also gave her kids a video they will cherish for generations. I still keep in contact with the groom, as we formed a friendship throughout the process that will always be special to me. I remember most weddings I have been a part of, but this one is etched in my heart forever.

So, that's why a wedding is important. To create a frozen moment in time that celebrates and honors the start of your marriage love story, with as many people there to support you in your journey as you desire. Because you and your spouse-to-be are worth it, and so is your matrimony.

Now, with that said, the bigger questions (especially since you have purchased this wedding-planning guide) may remain to be:

What type of wedding do you and your spouse want, and are you on the same page?

What is most important to both of you on your day, and if you don't agree on these non-negotiables, how will you compromise?

And finally, can you pull it off together or will you need help?

Actually, before I get to that, let's take a moment to talk about something else a bit more defining. No matter where both of you stand on your special day and your planning, how much of your imagined wedding day is based off of *unrealistic social media standards*?

Chapter 2

The Myth of Social Media (a.k.a. The Truth About What You See)

First, I'll state the obvious. What you see on social media is almost always highly-staged. Let me repeat: social media weddings are not necessarily real life. To add to that, I also don't believe weddings should be a competition sport. I really can't stress this enough, especially since I see so many of my couples wasting time and energy *worrying* about social media. So, let's take some time to debunk some of my favorite social media myths:

1) **Myth: Your event has to live up to some sort of social media standard or ideal.**

FALSE: Absolutely not. In fact, it simply has to live up to *your* expectations (and sometimes not even those). As I said before your event should capture the essence of your coupledom. It should speak to who you both are and how you came to be together. It should not be designed with social media at the center. None of those people peeping on your pictures today will be around in twenty, thirty, forty years. You and your love story will. Make your wedding matter to you.

2) Myth: Knowing how many followers a vendor has is important because if it's a lot, they've gotta be good.

FALSE: Not necessarily true at all. I mean, some are fabulous, I'm sure. But some great businesses have poured their hearts and souls into their services, rather than their social media presence. Those may have just as loyal and dedicated clientele, they just don't tout it on the internet. Also, you've heard about buying followers, right? If you haven't, well, now you have. It's a relatively common practice for businesses and people to do in order to seem like they have a larger realm of influence. The first sign of fake followers is generally a super low number of likes and comments per post, despite having a massive 'fan base.' Keep an eye out for it, and you'll see what I mean. And to be honest, it doesn't mean this business is acting shadily either. Maybe they just got caught up in the social media game, too.

Perfect example: a certain vendor I know and have worked with has approximately twenty thousand followers. That is a really solid amount, right? However, when this company posts something, I notice that even after a few days they only have 25-30 likes, and virtually no comments. This surely doesn't make sense, as I have a much smaller following and double the interactions on my posts. Consider the same company, but fast forward a few months: their followers have not changed much, but now their posts have a lot more likes within seconds of posting a photo.

I like to educate myself, so after witnessing this, I expanded their list of followers and found every person I clicked on was a ghost. Each account had no posts, no followers, and no following: bots. What I'm getting at is that a company's following doesn't determine its quality or worth. Consider that a highly creative, involved small business owner may not have the time or means to spend their energy on social media presence. They could be pouring their efforts into more important things, like their clients' weddings. That's how some of the strongest businesses have survived some of the toughest of times: word-of-mouth referrals, not social media. And while that may sound crazy, especially nowadays, I can personally attest to this.

Over the years I have built a successful business that has thrived because of my lasting relationships with clients and vendors. I make sure that my clients have an amazing experience and that they always remember me as a positive part of their wedding. I also always try to be easy to work with, play by the rules of every venue, and that the event day is all about the couple.

While I do try and post a quick photo or video clip on social media to show I am working and the quality of my work, I have found two things to be true. First, I do not have much time to post videos. Second, *many of my clients request we do not post their weddings*, which I have to respect. In the end, this forces me to focus my time on making sure my clients treasure what I create for them so much that they'll want to pass me along to their friends. And to their friends' friends.

Thus, when picking a vendor it's more important to keep in mind a business's quality of work than their thousands of followers you'll never meet.

3) Myth: Relatedly, a vendor's content reflects the quality of their services.

FALSE: This myth is based on many assumptions. It is also often based on flawless photographs or videos that have been curated to the nines at the cost of thousands of dollars.

When we look at a social media image we might see overflowing floral accents, perfect lighting, flawless makeup, and the most stunning outfits you've ever seen. These photographs include gorgeous backdrops, venues with views we all pray for, and *actual models* pretending to be getting married. What those images *don't show you* is how curated these series usually are. They are what we in the wedding industry call, "styled shoots." In essence, they're designed and displayed to be flawless, and generally feature models instead of real couples.

And unless you have an absolutely unlimited budget, no wedding day can live up to these limitless standards. So, if you're seeking a vendor based on a photo, I suggest reaching out to them and asking for more from the same event, or maybe even ones from past events in your area. Inquire if their social media content is from a styled shoot, and even if it is, derive some ideas for your big day from it. Just employ caution and perspective when you look at these stunning collaborations.

Also, keep in mind that even if your wedding ends up looking like a dream come true to you, your photographer won't necessarily have the time to get the absolutely perfect shot of every detail. Even if you can afford to pull out all the stops you see on social media, everyday weddings fall victim to the same rules as any day of the year, and things happen that can throw a wrench in your day at any point. If you've planned effectively you can still have a gorgeous, enjoyable event. It's just that chances are it's not going to look exactly like a curated photography session on social media.

4) Myth: If I follow every high-end vendor there is and take notes, my wedding is bound to be just as fabulous.

FALSE: Well, let me clarify something. *Your wedding will be fabulous regardless.* It is the event you've planned to celebrate your love. Even hiccups along the way don't cause for a bad day. But what can be pretty detrimental are unrealistic expectations. Following every high-end vendor for inspiration, while nice to look at, may not be that helpful dose of reality you need. The amount of money spent at some of these more lavish weddings, or even services donated at these styled shoots, can be absolutely astronomical. I know, I've been to all types of events and have seen *all types of bills*. I truly believe that aligning your vision with something outside of your budget may only serve to disappoint you.

I mean, imagine you find yourself looking to buy a car in a mid-level budget, but you've only taken the time to follow Rolls Royce, Ferrari, and Lamborghini. If your car budget is between $25,000 - $50,000 and the three companies you're getting inspiration from online don't offer a new car for less than $200,000 (a number that is over 4 times your budget), you're setting yourself up for failure. Or at the very least, some heavy disappointment. Similarly, someone once told me an excellent piece of advice.

"Your expectations must meet your budget, and your budget must meet your expectations."

In terms of social media, I truly suggest you use that rule of thumb as a tool. But like any tool, use it carefully and appropriately. Be sure to look discerningly for companies that post using varied methods of sharing (stories, reels, pictures, etc.), and seem to display authentic versions of their work. Like in any other realm, all vendors want to put up their most impressive work, but it's your job to seek content made with a realistic lens. Talk to the vendors and ask questions. And on the flip side, make sure to not dismiss a vendor's profile because they do not have a large following. There could be a variety of reasons for this, as discussed above, and it's important to keep this in mind.

Chapter 3

Budget... How Much & Who Bankrolls the Big Event?

You know me, I'll never mince words. So, here it goes: weddings are not cheap. In fact, some weddings set people back as much as a mortgage down payment might.

I've found that money and budgeting is always one of the most awkward conversations you'll have to host surrounding your nuptials. However, it's an important one, considering your event will be controlled by finances (to a certain extent). Which leads me to say that my first tip in terms of money is that I highly suggest having an in-depth conversation about your budget. Second, I recommend having things clearly laid out in writing (or a similar record), so there are no nasty turns along the way.

The first step in budgeting is to know exactly what you'll have to spend by accounting for where it will be coming from. Questions to answer would include, who is contributing to the budget? Are you throwing the wedding of your dreams as a couple, or are your parents pitching in? If so, how much can they each afford? I highly suggest having *separate chats* with each household, so as to not make anyone unnecessarily uncomfortable. Whatever that looks like or whatever needs to be done to put your families at ease, the important thing is that by the end of these talks you'll know what each person is willing to contribute to the pot.

Once that's decided, that will dictate quite a bit.

For example, I always suggest those getting married consider the fact that their venues should cost about fifty percent of their budgets. Now, that is certainly not an extremely rigid number. But with all the other items or services to purchase, rent, or hire for your event, choosing a venue with a larger portion of the budget can be dangerous.

Speaking of dangerously-growing budgets, here are some logical things to consider in terms of budgeting:

1. I strongly advise you to *not* start booking a venue or vendors without discussing your budget! Let's say you fall for a photographer that takes stunning photos and book them without hesitation, but then you realize their pricing chips away at your venue portion of the budget too much. It's important to get the budget talk out of the way before you sign away some of it.

2. Another great idea before booking any vendors or buying any wedding goodies is to make sure you talk about what's most important to you. Meaning, have a discussion with your spouse-to-be and those contributing to your budget about what they expect from or amidst the event. These expectations may dictate quite a few factors about your wedding, like where you have it, or how many guests you invite.

3. It's also important to keep in mind that (although parents or other relatives chipping in may not need to hear these *exact* words) **equal pay does not mean equal play.** What I mean by that is if your parents chip in the same amount of money as you and your betrothed-to-be, that doesn't necessarily mean they'll be given the same amount of clout in terms of the guest list or the decision-making processes. It is up to the couple to set realistic boundaries with each person contributing to the budget. I say that, especially in terms of parents, because I've found it necessary to host a clear discussion about what allowances might come with contributing money to the wedding.

Once you have decided on how much money you have to spend, then you should decide on a venue and vendors. Here are my generally foolproof, most common budget and vendor-related suggestions I give to couples who visit me:

1. As I said before, a general rule of thumb is your venue should be about 50% of your budget. Venue costs generally include a site fee, food, beverages, tables, chairs, and flatware (as funny as that sounds). There are ways to avoid spending that large of a portion of your budget on the venue, but without serious sacrifices in terms of your other needs or wants, it may be difficult to swing.

2. Next, your job is to figure out what other wedding-related services or items are most important to you. You may have addressed this with family in your earlier budgeting talks, but I think it's also important to have this discussion with your fiancee on your own time as well. It is *your day*, after all. In no particular order, other services to consider would include: coordinator, photographer, videographer, DJ/band, florist, attire, hair & makeup, invitations, officiant, cake, and favors.

3. I suggest you get quotes from several vendors you like in each category, so that you can determine how much you want to spend. Knowing the 'going' or average rate for a service or product really helps. A great related idea is to make an excel spreadsheet or similar document in which you can plug in various

prices and see how they interact with each other in order to remain within your budget.

4. I do highly caution you on "cutting" vendors that may actually be important. A much better option than eliminating services would be to keep all your desired vendors, and simply purchase a smaller package with each one. In the past I've experienced couples cutting videography "due to budget," which they almost always express disappointment about in the future. You can always opt for a smaller cake or less-inclusive photography package in order to hang on to video or other services.

5. Remember, weddings are large events with many moving parts. There are often additional costs that may come about. For example, extra rentals, dessert upgrades, a photo booth, guest favors, and transportation often add to the ever-growing bill. There is no exact math to figuring out what percentage you should spend on what. I just suggest leaving a little wiggle room in your budget for things that may arise that were originally unaccounted for.

6. Stay flexible and understand that weddings often require a sort of "budget bargaining." What I mean by that is illustrated in this anecdote: when my wife and I planned our

wedding, we decided together that we would save money on the appetizers, the bar, and the main course. Our thoughts were that appetizers get eaten no matter what, so we opted for less pricey ones. As for the bar, we felt the same, and chose a middle-of-the-road alcohol package. We decided together that we didn't need to supply everyone with top-shelf drinks all night. As for the main course, we chose a 'beef' instead of filet mignon. These three alterations saved us a few thousand dollars in the end, which was obviously well worth it. At the same time though, our bargaining and flexibility allowed us to avoid "cutting" anything out, too. That's why keeping an open mind about planning and budget strategies can surely help ease the stress of unmet expectations.

Another factor that often comes into play when talking money and weddings is the day of week on which you'll get hitched. While most weddings do occur on Saturdays, many also happen on Fridays and Sundays. As Saturday is the most popular day for a wedding, that day books up the fastest. It is also the most expensive. When looking at venues, consider asking about the cost of a Friday and/or Sunday wedding. You will typically find there is either a smaller minimum fee, or it is flat-out less expensive. Plus, not only can the venues be less expensive overall, but many vendors will have more wiggle room to give, as their main bread and butter is Saturdays. For example, my brother-in-law and his wife got married on a Friday, as did one of my close friends. Both of these events cost about twenty percent less across the board. When friends or clients ask about saving money on a grander scale, I always share the option of a Friday or Sunday event.

Allow me to share one last, very important budget-related piece of wisdom: nobody will leave your wedding saying, "Wow that was so beautiful! What a perfect day! Except, ya know, I really wish they had (insert some random appetizer, drink, or cow product)."

People are there to witness your matrimony and to have a blast celebrating, regardless of what you serve or how you decorate. At the end of the day, you will only plan one special day like this in your lifetime, and you want it to be lovely. It's not worth *over-expensing* yourself, but I always feel it is worth spending what you can afford to have a beautiful celebration of your love.

Chapter 4

Where on Earth Do You Get Hitched?

It's effectively one of your biggest questions from the start: *where* do you have your wedding?

I've learned that while some have thought about this their whole lives, others have no clue. Either way, in terms of options, you've got plenty. In fact, you've got a whole world full of them! Generally speaking there are two types of weddings. Destination weddings are hosted away from where the couple calls home, and are generally for those who love to travel, make a weekend of events, and/or just want to make an ever-growing guest list pare itself down naturally. On the flip side, maybe getting married in the local church or synagogue you grew up going to is most important to you. While there is no right or wrong answer to this *(again, this wedding should reflect you and your coupledom)*, let me share a few insights about both sides.

First, let's talk local weddings. Keeping it close can mean keeping it simpler, at least in some ways. To start, the

easier a venue is to get to for the bride and groom, the more
they may be able to peek in prior to their own event. Want
to spy what a wedding looks like there in real-time? A local
venue makes this so much easier. A wedding not far from
home also usually implies that most of your guests won't
have a long commute, and that most people won't need
to book hotel rooms. Sure, out-of-town guests will need
a place to stay no matter what, and sometimes even local
friends use weddings as an excuse for a hotel. However, if
you choose to have wedding-related group events amidst
your weekend, those invited can come and go more easily
when things are close to home.

Also, with a local wedding, it becomes somewhat easier
to hire vendors, as the venue you select will often provide
a list of suggested businesses they can vouch for. Nearby
businesses become easier for you to visit. Of course, you
can still be given a vendor list by your destination wedding
venue. Staying local just means your friends can share their
great vendor suggestions, too! Word-of-mouth is a great
way to find your vendors, and your loved ones will surely
know more professionals in your neighborhood. Another
benefit of using local vendors is that you won't be charged
any potential extra travel fees, which can become rather
pricy.

In terms of a destination wedding, consider that if
you live in Los Angeles and are planning a wedding in
Santa Barbara, Palm Springs, or Temecula, these are still
considered destinations. In other words, once a wedding

requires an overnight stay to attend, that becomes deemed a destination wedding. If it's hard for people to drive a few hours to your wedding and home on the same night, then it's still a destination wedding. Of course, a destination wedding can also require an airplane ride or any other major mode of transportation.

Thus, if you're planning a destination wedding, it's common to book or reserve a room block for guests at a hotel of your choice. Another pretty common task the bride and groom will have to complete (especially amidst a destination wedding) will be planning pre- and post-wedding events, such as a rehearsal dinner and day-after brunch. Finally, if people are schlepping somewhere for your wedding, it's also common practice to create 'welcome' bags for those staying in the hotel.

With all of that said, the number of people attending destination weddings is generally smaller than a local wedding, considering it often costs guests a much larger amount of money to attend. Travel costs, lodging, gas, parking, and gifts can add up pretty quickly. Thus, if you opt for a destination wedding, you may see a lot more invitation declines than you expected, especially the further you plan the location.

Still, I feel I should warn you, while some might pass all together, others will make your wedding their "vacation" for the season and even stay longer. I had a friend who got married in the Caribbean with the intention of hosting a smaller wedding. The bride and groom figured less people would be attending, so they opted for the hotel of their dreams, and went overboard on their venue costs. Well, it turned out that their guests had no problem missing work or taking their kids out of school. This led to over *eighty percent of their guests attending* and left the couple with one massive and unexpected wedding bill!

In general though, if you're afraid of your wedding being too big, a destination wedding is a great solution for cutting the list down. However, you know your guests better than I do, and I highly suggest you *never bank on assumptions*. You also can't have any expectations about who attends and who doesn't. Remember, to attend you're asking your guests to shell out money on what might include flights, hotels, meals, time missed at work, and possible childcare. So, when you have a destination wedding, you can truly have little to no guest-related expectations.

Now, in terms of what *type of venue* you should choose, you've got lots of choices.

1. At a *hotel*, there are built-in sleep options for your guests and less opportunity for drunk driving if you serve alcohol.

2. There are also venues strictly made for events or weddings, such as **banquet halls.**

3. For a homier feel, you may want to rent a home or private estate (a popular choice in Southern California).

4. Some resorts, hotels, halls, or homes can include all-inclusive packages. This is, in essence, another option in terms of venue (although there is an overlap).

Regardless of the exact venue, each has pros and not-pros (as I think it's all relative to each couple). While I cannot name them all, I hope my bits of insight will help you narrow down what type of venue you and your love would like.

Let's start with hotels. The largest perk about hotels is that they usually have everything you need already on their property. This would include rooms available for guests, a kitchen, bar, bathrooms, tables, chairs, etc. Now, while many people may have to rent their own supplies at other types of venues, hotels usually include them. On the flip side, the most popular concern about hotels is that this type of venue often holds multiple events at one time. While some couples do not care, others want their event to be the only one at this venue on their day for organizational purposes. This is a question you can ask the on-site planner or employee about.

If you are seeking a smaller, more intimate experience while still experiencing the perks of a designated event space, a banquet hall is a great choice. They are not generally attached to a hotel or lodging options for your guests, but they will often have the rest of what you're seeking in terms of food, drink, furniture, and more. You will still have to find a space for your out-of-town guests to stay, so picking a venue not far from hotel options is a good idea.

For those leaning towards an estate or private property, know that you will likely be paying a site fee to utilize the property. After that, everything else is your responsibility. This means you may need to have your caterer bring a kitchen, and you'll also need to rent bathrooms, chairs and tables. In essence, you might have to turn that historic home or seaside retreat you've selected in to a functional wedding space. Considering this, although an estate or at-home event can seem cost-effective, it often becomes more expensive than other options.

One last option you will come across is all-inclusive venues. These are wedding venues (usually hotels or resorts) that offer packages priced at a specific dollar amount per guest. This amount will include your site fee, dinner, drinks, D.J., photographer, officiant, florist and so on. Many all-inclusive places imply a destination wedding in places like Mexico or The Caribbean, but there are local inclusive places to be found as well. Like everything else, this has its pros and 'not-pros,' too.

All-inclusive venues are ready to go at any time and can churn weddings out with assembly-line precision. Which is perfect for a couple that really is *ready to get married* and has no interest in picking their own vendors. While your wedding will still be beautiful, a drawback is that all of their events tend to look very similar, with the exception of the attendees. The lower cost per guest also translates to the venue hiring less expensive vendors, which you may or may not be happy with in the end. To top it off, when it comes to all-inclusive venues, you do not typically meet with your vendors ahead of time; they are automatically booked by the venue. That means you also may not be given options to choose items such as flowers, lighting, photography style, etc, as these vendors generally pick them for you. Thus, those looking for a more personal wedding experience may be disappointed with an all-inclusive experience.

Something that can often effect which venue you select and where you choose to get married *is the time of year you're getting hitched.* I encourage my client-couples to consider this early in the planning process as well. You've gotta think about how the season and/or weather may play a role in your wedding day. What happens if you planned for an outdoor wedding and it forecasts rain? Does your venue have an indoor space in the event of inclement weather, and will there be another event happening there at the same time? Who would supply a tent if there is no inside option? In case you didn't know, a tent rental can cost over ten thousand dollars! Accounting for the unknown, as I discuss in the budgeting chapter, is always a great idea to be prepared.

I can recall only a few blustery, rainy events I've had to cover, as I'm located in Southern California. Two significant experiences come to mind. At the first one, the rain took us all by surprise. This meant the couple ended up having to get married inside instead of outside, which was modified by the venue relatively easily. The bride and groom remained totally relaxed, which I admired. But the bride's mother started to fret in an over-the-top way, *as if anyone could change the weather*. In the end, after some encouragement and distraction, the couple grabbed some umbrellas and we took some gorgeous, romantic shots of them outside. It truly was unique and beautiful, and only seemed to prove how important to your happiness it is to stay flexible.

On the flip side, another wedding that I will never forget was at what seemed like a pristine venue along the sunny Santa Monica coastline. After everyone trickled in (and literally minutes before the ceremony started), there was a huge downpour that lasted about an hour. The venue would not let anyone inside, and everyone (including grandparents and the vendors) sat outside in the rain. Once it stopped, the staff wiped the chairs, we trudged through the wet sand to the ceremony site, and *then* the wedding began. Now, while it all worked out in the end, the hour of rain surely put a damper on the day. My point is that although I do not know your location or venue, it is always good practice to ask your venue about weather and to be prepared for anything.

Now that I've gotten all of that out of the way, there are a couple things I want you to consider as you pull the trigger and book a venue. How exactly do you know a venue is the right one for you? Think about these factors as you select:

1. Location and the physical aesthetic of your venue control a lot. I would google images of a wedding at your potential venue. Can you see yourself having your wedding ceremony and nuptial photos taken there?

2. Each event space will have its own unique style and characteristics, especially if there are both indoor and outdoor areas to utilize. Does the look of the venue jive with your vision of your wedding? Are all of the areas you would use amidst your event functional for your guests?

3. Food and level of service are important to a wedding. You want your guests to enjoy what they are eating and who is serving it to them. I recommend searching for online reviews by past couples or wedding guests that speak about the quality of food and service at a venue or made by a catering service.

4. Lastly, as I said before, know your backup plan in the event of inclement weather *before you book*. Even at the most perfect location in the middle of summer, rain can occur. You do not want to be stuck without backup.

With all of that said, the last most common venue question I receive is about how my wife and I picked our venue. It was pretty simple, actually. While I had been to hundreds of venues all over Southern California, we had to think about what was most important to us. We wanted a place that was *local to our family*, as we had a handful of grandparents whom we didn't want to ask to travel. From there, I narrowed down a few venues for my wife to look at (and ultimately hoped she'd select my favorite, which I not so subtly pointed out to her).

Thankfully, she did and we went with a country club very close to our neighborhood. After having worked there many times, I fawned over the luscious grounds and the great food (yes vendor meals, too!), and appreciated the professionalism of how the director of catering ran all their events. I admit, knowing the inner workings of the venue helped, but an educated bride or groom has the potential to know as much as I do (especially after reading this book :-P).

In fact, our venue staff pretty much made me feel like a king (via the most expensive cheeseburger I've ever eaten). When we did our tasting, my wife chose salmon. Then they asked me which dish I wanted, to which I had to reply "a cheeseburger and fries." The planner definitely laughed, then asked me if I was serious. I was dead serious; they had the best burgers, which I had tried while golfing. Funnily, our guests watched me eat it at the wedding and were pretty jealous. But I don't regret a moment...except maybe I should have asked for a few extra pickles.

At the end of the day, we could not have been happier with our venue. I attribute that to picking a place we both loved for reasons we both appreciated. That's what it's all about.

Before I leave this chapter, I wanted to add a quick note about who hitches you. If you are religious, you will most likely have someone of that religion marry you such as a Pastor or Rabbi. However, many of the wedding ceremonies I've witnessed have no religion and the couple chooses to hire a wedding officiant. This person is hired, meets with said couple in person or over the internet and writes a ceremony tailored around the small bit they know. They do a great job and most are happy with their services. However at times, couples share the thought of missing the connection and they would prefer something more tailored to them. My suggestion becomes having a friend or family member marry them. In the past years, I have officiated a friend's wedding and my brother's wedding. These were two very powerful and exciting events for me. When asked, I gladly accepted and spent much time creating the perfect ceremony about the couple and using my knowledge from many points I've heard over the years. The results were unprecedented and the feedback was incredible. The two main things I notice when a friend or family member officiates are connection and attention. The connection comes from the closeness this person feels to the couple and in turn makes their ceremony more meaningful and powerful. The attention comes from the guests who are glued to this ceremony as they cannot wait to hear what is said next. Just another thing to consider but most people have someone in their lives who would do a phenomenal job. Each state and county is different but in most cases, this person can get a license to marry you online or in person. Like every other option, this comes down to personal preference.

Chapter 5

Do You Hire a Coordinator?

This is such a popular question it needs its own chapter. And before I dive into my answer, please take note that I use two different terms within this chapter, often going back and forth between coordinator and planner. There is a nuanced difference between the two: a coordinator is the person running the event on the day of, and the planner generally helps their couples plan *most everything* prior. To add, when you hire a planner, about 99% of the time they will be your coordinator on the wedding day as well (unless the venue offers one as part of a package).

While some of it depends on the scope and scale of your wedding, my professional opinion is that you should hire a coordinator for at least some portion of the day because there is a lot of value in professional coordination. Relatedly, below I'm breaking down your options in regards to the hired help you choose.

Option 1: Hiring a day-of coordinator only.

This is pretty much what it sounds like. A couple who has done most or all of their own planning and is looking to have a professional set of hands on the day of to lighten their load is most inclined to use this option. The coordinator will do some or all of the following: discuss their day-of duties in an initial meeting, attend and run your rehearsal, distribute your timeline to your vendors, supervise all setup, put out place cards, greet guests, line everyone up for the ceremony and grand entrances, and make sure the day runs smoothly. Furthermore, they will usually stay after to help pack up your gifts and even help load the car. Some venues will include a day-of coordinator in their wedding package or have an add-on option, which you may want to consider. Even still, other venues may *require* you hire a day-of coordinator, and in turn, should offer you a list of suggested vendors.

If day-of coordination is your only option, *it is truly worth every penny*. Otherwise, some ask their family or maid of honor to do all of this, but in my opinion that is *absolutely not ideal*, considering even a couple of these tasks will pull them away from your day too much. There are just so many moving parts in your day, I believe that hiring a day-of coordinator is absolutely worthwhile.

Option 2: Hiring someone for partial coordination.

This includes hiring someone to help plan your wedding at least a month before your event. A couple who has done most of the main components of planning (such as venue and some vendor selection), but still need help with other details, would find use in this package. Partial coordination includes the aforementioned day-of planning tasks. It also often includes tasks like creating a style for your wedding, referring any vendors you may still need, finalizing your budget, booking any last minute meetings, accompanying you to your tastings, making sure all vendor payments are made, and collecting insurance certificates from all vendors. This sort of package surely serves to offer more preparation and support for those couples who feel they need it.

Option 3: Hiring a coordinator for all planning angles or responsibilities.

Those who opt for this package often leave the wedding planning process with a new best friend. I suggest you find a planner you absolutely love and want to spend time with. That's because you'll be doing a lot of that: spending time together, trying to align your plans, and fine-tuning the design of your entire event. This would include everything I mentioned in both options one and two. It also includes unlimited contact (via e-mail, phone, or in-person), the process of researching and selecting a venue, creating a full budget, design renderings, vendor contract reviews, securing hotel room blocks, creating welcome bags for out of town guests, and pretty much everything else you can think of. This is the most inclusive coordination package with any company, and if you pick the right planner, the process is bound to be pain-free.

Surely, a deciding factor in the booking of a planner is cost. And the difference in price between the three packages above can be great. But where there is a will, there is a way. And if you feel the need to hire a planner, I suggest you bargain with your budget where you can. The help can be nearly invaluable. Then, once you've decided what kind of help you want, I suggest you decide who to hire. If you're stuck trying to figure out *who would be there for you to their best ability*, here is a list of useful questions to ask potential planners.

First, are you available on my selected wedding date?

Can you work within my budget?

Do you have insurance?

How many weddings have you planned before?

Have you planned any weddings held at our specific venue?

What can I expect from your planning process? How many meetings does this include, and what's your availability like?

Are there any common practices other planners do that you generally don't? And on the flip side, do you do anything other planners tend to avoid?

On the day of our wedding, will you be there?

Will any other staff be joining you to help?

What happens if you can't make it to our wedding because of extenuating circumstances?

Knowing the answers to these basic, preliminary questions (and any others that pop up naturally in the interview process) will allow you to get a feel for what type of planner or professional you're speaking with. Their answers will also give you a chance to learn about the person you're entrusting with your wedding. The more questions you ask, the better sense you'll gain. Don't be shy. And remember, no matter what extent you hire your planner for, having a professional coordinator as an advocate in any capacity is a win-win for you.

Chapter 6

Vendors, Vendors, Vendors

Quite honestly, the unsung heroes of your event will be your vendors, so choose them wisely. Not only are they the people who will bring your wedding dreams to life, but you will also have to feel comfortable traversing the process of wedding planning and execution with them from *start to finish*. And quite honestly, the last thing you'll want to waste your time doing on your wedding day is micro-managing a to-do list. In other words, finding the right vendors is truly the key to a successful wedding day because it is also the key to your ability to remain calm throughout what can be a very long planning process.

So, how do you find them? How do you know who to trust?

Like many things in life, I think a personal referral is always best. Not only can your friends and family speak from their own experiences, which allows you to learn what type of customer service you'll receive, *but they also know you*. They know what you like and how you operate, and most likely, what type of people would serve you best. So, my suggestion is to start there. Whether you reach out to friends who just got married, seek those employed in the wedding industry, or simply share a social media post requesting feedback, asking people who know you is the best first step.

Another great route is keeping an eye open at events you attend. Do you see floral arrangements you love or a planner who works her butt off to make the day feel seamless? Finding vendors at an event allows you to see them in action. It's good to keep in mind that even though you may see differences in your vision versus a friend's, that doesn't mean a vendor can't deliver what you want. It all comes down to personal preferences, quality, and communication. Just be sure to check with the couple to be positive that the quality of work you witnessed was the same reality behind-the-scenes.

As I shared in the opening of this book, I have been in this business since 1999 and happy clients who refer me to their friends is what has kept me going. I've been sent referrals by newlyweds, and also couples who used me ten years prior. I've been hired by people who met me at a wedding and liked how unobtrusive I was. And I've been hired by many friends of friends because my loved ones have vouched for my work ethic. Completely regardless of *how* the referrals come in, they have continued to because of my fun personality and high-quality product.

However, if your friends and family run dry on suggestions, or you just want a more objective referral, you can always ask your venue for vendors they can vouch for. Venues often possess vendor lists, which can be amazingly helpful, because they list their most trustworthy local vendors. Just be wary if your venue hands you a glossy, brochure-like booklet with information about their property, and an included list of vendors. Many times these consist of vendors that pay to advertise, and the venues only refer these people because they've spent money. At times, they might not have even worked with them yet. It's important to remember that flashy paraphernalia doesn't mean a quality job will follow. Call around and ask questions to get a better sense of a vendor's professionalism and product.

Another route, which many of you may select, is asking the coordinator you've hired for their best, most fitting suggestions. They'll know the ins and outs of the vision you're building together, and how to make it come to fruition most smoothly. You can also ask the other vendors you have hired that you know and trust.

Of course, there are also thousands of online reviews available to read. There are even wedding websites designed to give newlyweds a space to review their vendors. If you employ caution and skepticism, you can surely read these. I just like to remind people that these reviews can be biased, especially since you don't know if your expectations align with those of the reviews writers.

One more painfully popular question I get from my clients is whether they should use a DJ or a band. Of course, there are many factors which could determine which selection you go with. Some people love to have live music as they feel that brings the party truly to life. Others like the idea of a DJ mixing music, because they typically possess a larger variety of song choices. A realistic deciding factor could be price. Prices of both can vary greatly, but a band will usually run at least four times the cost of a DJ. I'm sure many of you looking into a band will be pretty surprised at how expensive they can be. However, you need to remember that this includes each member of the band, sound technicians, someone to bring all the equipment, mixing board(s), and so much more. A DJ usually brings his own equipment and perhaps one assistant. Like everything else in this book, most things come down to personal preference as well as budget.

My wife and I had one band in mind while planning our wedding. We were so impressed with their presence and how lively their events were. But at the end of the day, they were out of our budget. We ended up hiring the DJ, and we even paid for an hour of overtime at the reception because the party was going so strong. We also made sure to incorporate a live trumpet player in our ceremony as my wife walked down the aisle with her dad; that was our budget-friendly compromise to keep ourselves happy. Should you enjoy the aspect of live music like we did, you can always add live music to your processional, recessional, and/or cocktail hour. I've also seen other weddings host an artist to perform a first dance or parent-dance song. Really, it's your preference and pocketbook. I ultimately say, as I often do, go with your gut. If you like a vendor and you feel they will truly go above and beyond to deliver what you are seeking within your budget, hire them. I say that because I find comparing vendors is nearly impossible. The process is less like comparing apples to apples, and more like comparing apples to automobiles. Vendor prices differ greatly, but so can their designs, business practices, and credos. Thus, the most important things truly is how they fit in to your budget, and how supported they will make you feel before and on your wedding day. Everything else is incidental and subject to change.

For example, during one of my weddings, the bride quickly realized there was a mix-up with her bouquet. It had actually been left behind. To make matters worse, the florist had already hightailed it to another event. So, the coordinator quickly sprang into action. She sent one of her assistants to a local market to gather some flowers fit for a bridal bouquet. It took her some time, but she was able to design and deliver it before it became an issue. Talk about on the fly!

I have watched vendors get stains out of a wedding dress, switch set-ups around to accommodate last minute guests, kick out wedding crashers, calm angry parents, control a crazy bridal party, pick up food from a restaurant outside the venue for a guest with an allergy, and even lent a diamond wedding band for ceremony use when the rings were forgotten. These Hail Mary-throwing vendors are the angels of the wedding industry.

On the opposite end of the spectrum, I've attended and worked a few weddings at which a vendor has been a no show, or called out of a wedding last minute. I know this may worry you as you read, but it is *very rare* and most companies would have backup for such a situation. However, on a few occasions the couple was left high and dry. But in stepped the coordinator, who was able to reach out to someone in their network and get a replacement on the same day. Even I have even been called on for immediate video production! It takes a village, even to get married.

As I said before, *who* you hire is relative to your budget, planning, and goals. But *how* you hire them is important, too. I always suggest asking potential vendors lots of questions in order to gain a stronger semblance of their work and practices. That way you'll likely avoid the nightmare of a flaky vendor or other potential issues. Here is a list of questions fit to ask any wedding-related business you're thinking of hiring (although a few may have to be altered vendor-to-vendor):

What is your payment schedule?

What sort of deposit do you require?

How do you request final balances are paid?

Is there sales tax on part or all of your services?

Should we need to cancel, what is your cancellation policy?

Do you offer any discounts for a Friday, Sunday or mid-week wedding?

What payment methods are accepted? Are there fees for credit cards?

Do you have insurance?

We have met with you. Are you personally going to be at our event? If not, who will be?

Can any other charges arise beyond what is quoted?

Do you require a vendor meal?

Should something happen to you, do you have a backup person who would show up?

Have you worked at our venue before?

If a product is delivered, how long do you anticipate we will have to wait to receive it?

Chapter 7

Your Only Memories, Video & Pictures

As I have spent the majority of my life being a videographer, I have a lot to say on this topic. First off, with no hesitation on my part, *YES*, you need a wedding video. I sometimes hear couples ponder whether they need a videographer or not, and I can't even begin to understand where this thought process came from.

According to several studies I have read, passing on a videographer is the *number one* regret wedding couples have. Having photos is simply not enough because, while still images can be an art form, the best photos cannot produce sound. How could you have the biggest celebration of your life and have no way to ever hear your vows or toasts again? You'll never be able to witness the live movements of your first look, the opening sequence of your first dance as a married couple, or the sweet, stolen glances during the cake cutting. These are the priceless moments that allow you to relive your wedding day over and over again.

Sure, a photo can capture a father-daughter dance, or the slicing of the cake. But will the photos capture the intricacy of the spins you were rehearsing for weeks prior, or the smear of cake the groom licks off the bride's face? No. There is so much *spontaneity* that ends up happening throughout the wedding day that a videographer truly captures.

I know what you're thinking... Spontaneity? After all this chatter about planning? But it's true. Amidst such a calculated, orchestrated event, it's these off-the-cuff memories that make it most memorable. One of my favorite things to remind my clients is that just like in life, unexpected things happen at weddings, too. Sometimes that's to warn them to have less expectations, but most of the time it's because the majority of the magical moments of a wedding are those that are unplanned. And those unplanned occurences are the ones that can be hard to capture without a videographer.

Also, imagine being able to show your children your wedding video one day. I've shown our kids our video, and it is the best feeling ever. Quite honestly, that is also my favorite piece of feedback I receive from my clients. I know the value of my work when they share a snippet of their kiddos watching their wedding video, or more specifically, send me a video of their kids asking, "Where am *I*?!"

When I receive calls and emails thanking me for the last live memory of a family member or friend, I can't help but feel so much pride. In fact, as I mentioned before, my best friend passed away about a year after my wedding, and it's so touching to see him in our video. My wife and I still sit in bed and watch our toasts from time to time. One of our favorite things to do is to watch my grandparents share words of wisdom. And nothing brings my wife to tears faster than watching her dad, whom we lost seven years after our wedding, make a toast to our promising future.

I'll take it one step further, although I apologize for getting even more personal. In September of 2019, my mom told me that my grandfather was going to pass very soon. As he was ninety-two years old, it wasn't quite a shock that his time was running out. But I recall one night after my wife went to sleep, I felt compelled to head downstairs and turn on our wedding video. I fast-forwarded directly to the rehearsal dinner speeches, which we hired someone specially to record.

That evening, I took the time to relive my grandfather's speech in particular. It was incredible to watch him talk. He offered a few funny anecdotes, and also many more loving stories about me. Then I turned off my television and called my mom to let her know what I was doing. I'm not sure why, but it seemed imperative to share that with her. But when she picked up, I could hear her sniffling on the other line.

It only took her a few beats for her to share that my grandfather had passed a few minutes earlier. I cannot even begin to describe how impactful it is to know that as he took his last breaths, I was listening to him speak. But the power of that experience will never leave me. And that's just my personal experience.

One time, after an extensive meeting, a bride chose not to hire us. However, as her wedding day grew closer, her desire to book a videographer became more nagging. Not too long before the wedding, she finally chose to hire us. Part of her deciding factor was that her dad was not well. But honestly, no one would have known because he was a rockstar on the big day.

That day, her father was present and dancing, smiling and beaming the entire way through. However, he unfortunately passed shortly after the wedding. The bride actually took the time to call me to let me know that before he passed, the family flew to his home on the East Coast and laid in his bed watching the wedding video. They were able to watch their ceremony entrance, those special minutes walking down the aisle together. They saw him make a wedding toast for the couple. They relived their special father-daughter dance. And to know that I had a part in bringing together a family for some of its last whole, heart-warming memories is incredible. Chilling at times, but moving, nonetheless. They will have this memory forever, and I will know I helped prolong it, too.

In short, take my word, *you will watch your video*. If not right away, there will be a time you will play it. And never for one second will you think, "Honey, we really should not have spent money on a videographer." *Which is priceless!* All these cherished moments, especially the ones captured via video, literally freeze our loved ones in time, forever.

Now that, we've gotten that out of the way, let's get to a little more of the nuts and bolts about wedding videos. In regards to style, there are basically two: videographer and cinematographer. I do not want to get too technical, but a videographer will capture your event with one camera in its basic form, while a cinematographer will usually direct the couple and capture more sweeping movements and such.

Almost all videographer and cinematographer packages will include some length of a highlight video. Most of the time this will be anywhere from three to eight minutes, as each company will differ. In a simple sense, a videographer is a bit more documentary-like and focuses on recording the event. Personally, I have been including a long form-edited video with highlights since I started my company; some call this a documentary edit or 'doc edit.' A cinematographer is more about the art of making a movie. Cinematographers will usually include a longer "film" in their packages, which could be in the ten-to -thirty minute range. *The most important thing to know when signing with a videography company is what you will receive as part of your package.*

Many times couples will say they are not interested in a "long, boring video" and state they will never watch it. But when it's **your** personal video, you *will* want to watch it. There is so much missed by the couple that a longer video of some sort can come in handy. Consider that your ceremony is about 20 minutes long, but your videographer provides a 5 minute highlight. Do the math, and it's easy to realize the shorter your video is, the more you lose out on your wedding. Thus, some sort of longer video is crucial.

If you are in love with a company that only provides a highlight, make sure to ask about the possibility of other footage. Just be careful of "raw footage," as is it exactly that. If a company offers "raw footage," that means the video is untouched in the editing booth. Which means you're receiving hours of unedited action. At times, they may take three shots of the dress, but after editing will only use one in the final video. If you receive raw footage, you will see all three.

All of that is to say, if and when you hire a videographer, make sure you know very clearly what they'll be giving you in the end. Before you book, you can even ask vendors to send you a longer video they've created, or a longer piece of one, such as the entire ceremony. This will really help give you an idea of what you will receive from this company.

Now that I've got that out of my system, in terms of finding a great wedding photographer, my advice is to hire someone you would want to hang out with. In fact, that remains to be true for any of the vendors you hire, but especially for those that will be by your side most of the day. A good personality is key because you want this person to make you feel very comfortable and natural in your photos. Of course, it helps to know if their photography demonstrates a similar style to the one that you are looking for.

For example, some photographers shoot with a very photojournalistic point-of-view, which generally has less posing and more candid photos. Others may take more stylized pictures by setting up poses and using lights and flashes. Still, other photographers process their images in post-production, which have a similar effect as those on social media. For such an image-based vendor, I suggest searching databases and finding local photographers you admire in your area.

Before you book though, I highly recommend meeting with this person or studio in the flesh (or video chat, if necessary). I also suggest seeing photos of a few real weddings they have photographed. That is because there are so many parts to a wedding day. You want to make sure this professional can capture it all: the ceremony, family portraits, dancing shots and so much more. I always tell clients to ask to see a ceremony in its entirety, as well as the audience's reactions amidst it, before you sign with a photographer. You will want to see what that looks like from their brand. Are the people in focus or blurry? Are their skin tones smooth or blotchy? Are the pictures telling a story in a fun way or are they generic and boring? Can you imagine swapping out those happy people for your friends and family? Sure, the posed moments you're seeking are important, but only account for a small percent of the day. You might hang them in your home and use them for "thank you" cards, but the candid captures will be what you truly fall in love with. Always ask to see a photographer's less-posed shots, too.

Similarly to when you hire a videographer, it's important to know what kind of coverage is included in a photographer's packages, and what included products you'll be receiving. A common practice is charging what is called a "coverage fee." This means they will photograph up to a certain amount of hours and provide the photos afterwards; typically these don't include product. Photographers' fees can also include things like albums, wall portraits, a sign-in book, canvases, your engagement shoot, etc. With that said, my biggest piece of advice is to *try to avoid being blinded by products in a photography package.*

Let's say you are shopping around and find two photographers you adore. But one includes an engagement session, wedding album, and one canvas print, while the other only includes the coverage fee. That's when you have to backtrack to what drew you to them in the first place, because printing wedding goodies later is totally possible, and sometimes even a way to save money. You should also really consider their actual photos and personality. Which one jives with you and your vision more? Which photographer do you want to be a part of your wedding *all day long?*

Time and time again I have heard from brides that chose to hire a photographer that wooed them with product rather than quality pictures. Those same brides often consistently report that they were unhappy with the photographer's performance, which leads to minimal excitement about receiving their photos. In the end, that leads to even more disappointment because if you've been wrangled in by a larger package that includes product, but you're not impressed with the images, what is the product even worth? These are your wedding photos and you want to love them as much as you loved your wedding day! You can always buy an album or prints after the fact, but you can never retake these once-in-a-lifetime pictures.

My overall advice in terms of media-based memories? Do some thorough research on your potential videographer and photographer because who you choose will be an investment in your future memories. It really doesn't matter if you choose a full package or simple coverage. What will ensure your happiness with your images and video will be choosing the right person and effectively communicating your needs to them.

Chapter 8
Everything Bridal Party

I keep reiterating that your wedding is about you and your love story, right? Well, here's a revolutionary thought I usually share that tends to blow the minds of my brides and grooms: *your wedding party is (mainly) about you, too.*

That is to say, selecting the bridal party is a big job, but it is also a personal one. You're meant to choose people who mean the most to you, the ones you couldn't imagine getting married without, and who you want to share in all your festivities. This is not about childhood friends you haven't seen in years, or who your parents want in your wedding party. This is *about your relationships.* The people who you know, trust, and love.

There is no rule that says just because you were in a person's wedding that you necessarily need to have them in your wedding. Relationships and bonds are unique; you may be someone's best friend, but you may have even closer friends. Relatedly, just because someone is family, that does not give them an automatic bridal party invitation. A bridal party can consist of siblings, cousins, or friends. I mean, it could even include co-workers, if you feel so inclined. I have even seen a mother getting married and her daughter stood beside her as her maid of honor; anything goes as long as it is what you want. Again, what I am getting at is this is about you and who is most important in your lives.

Another key piece of advice I like to offer is to avoid getting caught up in having an even number of bridesmaids and groomsmen. It is possible for the bride or groom to have a different number on their side. Having someone walk down the aisle alone, even having two groomsmen with one bridesmaid, or vice versa is totally okay. *Again, there are no rules to this whatsoever.*

Relatedly, I recall a certain bridesmaid at one of my past weddings making the day all about her. All throughout hair and makeup time, she had something to say about everything. She shared things she had done on her own wedding day, from photo-posing ideas to unrelated, mundane anecdotes. Everything she did or said was related back to her own special day. To say that the bride was not happy is an understatement. I recall asking the bride if I could politely request that her bridesmaid share a little less, so the photographer could get more done. The bride quickly said yes and thanked me. She followed up with letting me know that this specific bridesmaid had talked about weddings non-stop since her own engagement *years prior.* The bride also admitted she had seen the red flags, and wished she would have left her out of the bridal party. So, my first no B.S. rule of wedding parties is to avoid picking party people to please others. At the risk of sounding redundant, I will remind you: you do you. I cannot tell you how many times I've seen brides or grooms invite bridal party members out of "duty," which often becomes an issue later for various reasons. Why invite conflict by doing something disingenuous surrounding *your day to keep someone else happy?*

Another thing I feel that is very important to discuss in terms of wedding parties is cost. While it is a huge honor to be in either party, it presents extra duties and costs for both the couple-to-be-married and for their bridesmaids and groomsmen. Bridesmaids will likely be responsible for showering the bride, planning the bachelorette party, and purchasing and/or renting clothing for the event. Groomsmen have most, if not all, of those duties, too. Sometimes participants also have to shell out money for wedding night accommodations, hair, makeup, and other services or products.

You might choose to absorb some of those costs, like hair and makeup, or you might not. Just know it is also customary to buy a thank you gift for all those that do participate in your bridal party. Their gifts do not need to be large by any means, but they should be thoughtful. Personalized keepsakes used the day-of your wedding that can be reused at other times work great. I've seen couples gift customized glassware, robes, shoes, ties, tote bags, etc., all of which are greatly appreciated. However, I always remind clients and friends to keep these costs in mind while planning their wedding, as they definitely add up.

Speaking of wedding duties, who doesn't love a great bridal shower? How about a bachelor or bachelorette party? It's best that all of these pre-wedding events (except for the rehearsal dinner) should take place about one to three months before the big day. Sure, these preceding parties are memorable and magical for the person getting married, but they're also great for the wedding parties, too. They are a chance for all to get involved, and for many to make new friends, or become closer to existing friends. Hosting them with enough time prior to the wedding ensures that your guests will have more time to meet and bond, and you'll have more time to get organized by the big day.

I won't bore you with stories or preferences in terms of wedding events, because I want to leave all the planning to you. And if I'm being truly honest, I could probably write a second book on bachelor and bachelorette parties. Also, sometimes I consider these parties to be even more personal than the wedding; they're your last hurrah with some of your best friends. They should be fun in the most responsible and cost-effective way as possible, but they should also be *totally you*. Whatever makes you happiest and your friends comfiest, just go for it.

In terms of pre-wedding parties (for both women and men), there is no golden rule about timing. Showers generally take place one to three months before the wedding. It may be thrown by a family member, or a member of your wedding party. It is generally a group effort to share ideas and coordinate the shower, but it all really depends on what the bride wants, or what people offer to do.

Remaining on the subject of costs, let's talk attire. I know in terms of dresses, *just the alterations* can be quite expensive. If you have many people out of town, choosing a chain with locations all over can be helpful. Chain stores also generally carry varied sizes and styles, which will allow you to find more potential styles to fit each one of your unique bridesmaids. Everyone will appreciate feeling represented and comfortable in the dress search. They will also appreciate if you consider *the cost of the dress(es)* when choosing, because their pocketbook will be effected greatly by this entire wedding process; chain stores often boast the most cost-effective dress options, too.

But I'd like to make it clear that this consideration should not only take place when it comes to the ladies. You'll also need to opt whether you'll make the gentlemen *rent or buy*. When I was planning my wedding I asked everyone to purchase suits because I found it would be much cheaper. When I did my research I saw that tuxedo rentals were about two hundred fifty dollars. From experience, I know if any part of it said suit or tux is missing when returned, it can be very expensive. So instead, I found a three day suit broker. I searched through the store, picked a suit I thought was sharp, and sent the information to all my guys. As it tends to be the case with those kinds of places, the turnaround time was pretty quick.

In the end, I was able to find slim fit suits for ninety-nine dollars each. Once the shirt was added, the whole thing cost them about one hundred-thirty dollars. Some of them chose to meet with me on a specific day, and others who could not make it went in on their own and just gave my name to pick up their suit. It worked really well for us, and everyone included left happy. Plus, all of them owned a great suit they could wear again and again!

Like the rest of the planning, wedding party details and minutia should be left up to you, your spouse-to-be, and those involved. But truly, you should embrace everything that makes you and your friendships special in this process. There's no reason you *have to* have a traditional shower, bachelor, or bachelorette party.

Chapter 9

Who Gets an Invitation?

The guest list: let's get to it. And yes, I'm going to be extra blunt about this topic, considering it remains near and dear to my heart, and because *every single couple* has the conversation of who they should and should not invite. But what is the etiquette, or protocol, if you will?

As you ponder the people in your life, you might find yourself wondering if you should invite certain categories of loved ones, like your childhood friends. The more you think about them, you start considering their parents. And what about your boss? Especially if you've worked at the same place for a long amount of time, you might even be tempted to invite your co-workers. What about Sally? You have been friends with her for what feels like forever, even though you haven't seen her in a while.

Thus, the question naturally arises, "Who do you want to be present for your big day?" But there are so many more underlying questions that influence that decision, or may even be better to ask yourself to begin with.

Like, "Who have we seen in the last *six months?*" or some other set time frame you and your partner decide on.

Finding a parameter like that encourages a rigid boundary within your planning. It also surely helps you stay on budget. If you don't try to wrangle in your count, it's easy to fall into the trap of inviting *far* too many people. The question I ask my clients is if they're contemplating someone who they *do not* regularly spend time with, what is their connection to them? How important is it to have them present as they get married, or are they considering inviting them as a means to preserve a relationship they fear could end if they don't?

If it's the latter, let me share this: anyone whose feelings about you are as fragile as a paper invitation shouldn't receive one. Those who truly love you and want to see your marriage succeed should be able to consider that wedding budgets are fragile, too. Costs can run high rather quickly. Inviting someone to your wedding is less important than investing in your future, right? And hey, if you feel you absolutely have to invite them, maybe they should be on the list. *Maybe.*

In this vein, there will surely be quite a few guests you'll want to share the day with, but what about *their dates?* In terms of 'plus-ones' or dates, my professional opinion is that I would seriously stay away from giving people an open invitation to bring them. This is for several reasons. First, as we discussed in earlier chapters, when each guest can cost you anywhere from thirty to two hundred and fifty dollars, it becomes very easy to spend unnecessarily. Especially if a rule for date invites isn't implemented. I mean, imagine if you had ten friends who each asked to bring a date, and you say yes to each one without any prior parameters. That's an extra $300-$2,500 that could be spent somewhere else. Thus, allowing everyone a date can be absolutely cost-*ineffective*.

But more importantly (and let's be totally real) I have seen how most, relatively anonymous plus-ones act at the reception. Take my word for it, you will be upset you allowed them there when you see your pictures and video. For some reason most plus-ones take an elegant event and turn it into a college party. Perhaps it's because they aren't necessarily there to be present to witness your new union take place. They're really only there to take full advantage of your open bar and unending shrimp cocktail appetizers.

In short, my advice is to only allow guests to have plus-ones if they are in serious relationships. I know, even that term leaves too much room for interpretation. What I always suggest to my clients is if someone is married or engaged to be so, it is absolutely appropriate to invite their partner. Beyond that, things are dictated by your own preference. You can make the rule that if you haven't met their partner more than five times, you'd rather not include them. On the flip side, I've known couples to tell their friends and family that if they have been with their significant other as long or longer than the betrothed, dates were welcome. Any way you slice it, it's your decision. My best advice is to make a firm choice and stick to it because guest lists grow much faster than you think.

Another big question I get about the guest list revolves around kids. My thoughts are that weddings and children are an interesting combination. Little ones are super cute in photos and always make for the most adorable 'walking down the aisle' vignettes, but I think you might want to stop there. By that, I mean consider leaving the littles ones' participation out of the ceremony, or at least the reception. Please remember I have kids that I love intensely, so this is not a biased opinion. Of course, it really does depend on your younger guests' ages, manners, and whether the parents have the means to hire a babysitter or some type of help (so they can enjoy the wedding). But I have a few basic reasons for this stance.

First, the parents of the little ones are going to be incredibly occupied, especially without hired help. And if it is important enough to have your kids' friends there, it's probably even more important to have their parents happy and present. Let's be real, that's not terribly likely to happen if their kids are there. Secondly, having the kiddos at the ceremony is one thing. I truly do believe it honors the union of two families and the generational aspect of marriage. But as soon as the kiddos toddle out on to the dance floor at the reception, people flock and all cameras are now focused on the little ones. While that is seriously cute, the wedding is about the couple and should not revolve around the first time a child is "dancing." I have even seen newlyweds and guests grow upset that there isn't physical space for them to dance because too many people crowd around to watch the kids.

In my opinion, my brother really nailed the whole 'kids-at-your-wedding' thing. By then, I had already worked events for years and knew the safest drill so that my wife and I could enjoy ourselves. His nuptials were at a beautiful hotel with comfortable rooms; we were fortunate enough to be able to book two rooms that were attached, one for the girls and one for us. Then we asked a close family friend of ours (who was not invited to the wedding) to watch the girls. Our twins were present for all formal photos, and were also given the honor of walking down the aisle with my wife as the flower girls. The moment that was over though, we knew our little ones would not sit still for much more, so our friend stepped in to help. She took the twins back to the hotel room afterwards and enjoyed some room service and fun activities we had brought with us. This made it so the kids were not the center of attention, and also so my wife and I could enjoy the wedding, as we were both in the bridal party. I am a firm believer that there are always creative solutions to every issue that *may arise.*

A final, somewhat stress-inducing reality of the 'guest list chat' is pleasing family. And I'm going to get straight to the point, as I usually do.

Brides and grooms ask me about divorce all the time, too.

I mean, not theirs, of course. But we live in a society where there are many divorced parents (I've experienced three in my immediate family alone), and I believe you need to consider this when making your guest list. Since each parent or set of parents may now have different circles of friends, many times they might want to extend invites to all of them.

This is another area where I suggest coming up with a concrete way of discerning who gets an invite and who will have to just understand. One thing to do is discuss this early with your parents. You don't want to potentially hurt feelings or rock the boat too close to the event. Promoting an open avenue of communication from the get-go is essential. Also, take the time to make it very clear to each parent how many invites they are uniquely receiving, and who *you* may *not* want to be included in that group.

I experienced this surrounding my wedding. My mom wanted many of her and her husband's friends to be present at our wedding. When I told her that I have only met some of them a few times, and that I did not want to be introducing ourselves to people at our wedding, she started to understand. Especially because at the end of the day, it was *our wedding*, not hers. But no matter our reasoning, being clear and concise helped all parties involved.

After some time we ended up compromising. My mom and step dad held a small barbecue at their home a few weeks after the wedding. It was super casual, we made sure to specify we didn't want gifts on the invite, and the day was filled with nothing but pure love. People do really understand there is a limited amount of guests and the list needs to stop at some point, especially if you include them in a different way, or communicate your needs clearly.

Pretty simple, huh? Ha!

Chapter 10

The First Look

"Should I see my spouse before the wedding ceremony?"**

You'd be shocked at the number of times I've been asked this, and what a hot topic it is. I discuss it with *almost every client*. Thus, I've given it its very own chapter, so you can easily pop back and reread it if needed. And truly, the answer to it comes down to personal preference. But how on Earth are you supposed to make an educated decision if you don't know both sides of the coin, so to speak?

Well, first off, a first look constitutes seeing each other for an often-documented glimpse *before* the ceremony takes place. Not planning for one means you will snag your first glimpse of your spouse-to-be all dolled up at the start of your wedding aisle. And I will state that if not seeing each other is based upon a *religious reason*, then by all means, don't peek.

But let's look at the logistical side of things:

When a couple chooses to avoid doing a first look, this means the earlier hours of their wedding that would be used for preparation and pictures will only be used to capture separate images of wedding parties and families. That is to say getting ready will remain disconnected the entire time prior to the wedding, as well as during family portraits. At that point, the ceremony will begin with you and your future spouse still having not seen each other.

Now comes the hard part.

After the ceremony, cocktail hour begins! Amidst this time, since you didn't take your couple photos, joint family photos, or bridal party photos earlier, this is the time to do it! You'll have the span of cocktail hour, which is generally about sixty minutes, give or take a little bit. During that time someone will have to wrangle everyone up and squeeze in the pictures that you missed out on taking before. *This will leave you virtually zero time to visit with guests at that point.*

Here are some important factors to consider as you decide about your first look:

1. *If things are running late, the first thing to get cut is the coverage of the couple.* This is because, while it is your event, you will be the most constant thing there. A photographer will likely have less trouble both finding you and keeping you at your wedding throughout

the night. Family members and the bridal party are a whole other story. The herding of all the family and bridal party is always a daunting task, as everyone wants to visit. I mean, your mom's been waiting for this day forever, and now she wants to run around and visit with her friends. And the bridal party members? They're definitely ready for a drink, a few appetizers, and maybe a hug from their husband after the long day they've had. Which means you run the risk of missing people, or even frustrating family and friends because they can't just go enjoy themselves.

2. *If first look photos are captured prior to the ceremony, there is generally time to touch-up your makeup or looks before the ceremony begins.*

3. *From a videographer's perspective, cell phones are a pain.* They often impede us from getting the angle or shot we want when Aunt Sally has her tablet out, filming from the center of the aisle. Of course, there will be a good deal of photos taken from start to finish, but you will find that there is a shockingly low amount compared to what you imagined there might be. Having more people present while these shots are trying to be obtained (i.e. during the ceremony or after cocktail hour) always

adds more difficulty. It also often knocks the photographer off their very regimented schedule (for a typical wedding day schedule, see the next chapter). Having time for coverage beforehand eliminates some of this professional stress, too.

4. If you do a first look, *there's time to do whatever pleases you after the ceremony*, like attend cocktail hour, get alone time, or anything that suits your fancy. This usually gives time for the bride to bustle as well.

5. *The first look is intimate, special, and typically emotional.* It truly is the only real alone time a couple has on their wedding day and it is **magical**. Did I say that? Yes, MAGICAL! You have time to really take in that dress, the silky tux, and professional makeup. You can embrace each other in a real hug, a kiss, and a deep breath because it is *almost* wedding time. I mean, you've never seen a couple hug down the aisle, have you? That personal, intimate time really does make for a more relaxed, mellow bride and groom.

6. If you've taken the time to arrange that little moment before the madness truly begins, then not only have you seen each other, but your *anxiety is infinitely lessened, too.* The intense

build-up has dulled now that you have seen your love, and you're ready for the day. This also gives you more time with each other and your bridal party, which causes a natural glee that truly shows in your photos and video.

I surely don't know about you or your priorities, but my wife and I both went into our wedding knowing *we wanted to party* once the reception started. So, we opted for a first look, and I couldn't contain my tears. Fast forward to the ceremony, and I *still* cried the whole time she walked down the aisle. Absolutely nothing took away from that moment of her gliding towards me down the aisle. And we were thrilled to have the extra, posing-free time to spend at cocktail hour.

My clients who walk in and stalwartly say, "No Brian, we are not doing a first look," thank me the most.

I ask if I might share my opinions, the same that I shared above. And almost one hundred percent of them change their minds. I mean, it's no secret that I am a huge fan of the 'first look.' Still, as I said before, everything in this book truly *comes down to personal preference.*

Chapter 11

The Timeline (with samples)

They say "timing is everything," and after spending decades in the wedding industry, I know virtually nothing to be truer in my field. So, let's keep that in mind as we continue this conversation about your day. Your wedding timeline will dictate when things happen, how smoothly the event runs, and oftentimes, how much fun is allowed.

Before I dive in though, a few tips.

First, make sure you have your finalized timeline written out very clearly. This way, not only do your vendors know what's going on beat-by-beat, but you do as well. Just know that the actual design of your specific wedding timeline can be written with the help of your coordinator or on-site coordinator (many times I even help my clients with this). I would highly suggest when this is written that you at least seek the advice or input of *your photographer and/ or videographer as well.* They will let you know how much time they need for certain segments of the day (most of these being pre-ceremony), such as getting ready portraits, wedding parties and family. Their series of events or needs will dictate much of the rest that you have to plan.

It's also important to keep in mind that you will want to *keep some extra time as a buffer* throughout the event for things like makeup touch-ups, bustling of the dress, running behind, and eating. Heck, sometimes the bride or groom just need a few minutes away from the action. Consider the quote "life is what happens when you're busy making other plans." This is especially and painfully true on wedding days. Despite spending months planning the timing and order of operations, things will always go awry. Usually they're minute details, but still, with so many spinning plates a small change could translate to bigger ones down the road. That means it's important to stay relatively flexible, and avoid becoming too transfixed with the set times you *have* designated. The flow of things is more important than the rigid timing of things. You won't remember if you started appetizers late, but you'll definitely remember if you don't get family photos with your parents.

Regarding rigidity, I also recommend avoiding getting ready too far in advance. Makeup and hair are generally some of the first steps on your big day. But if something delays the onset of your schedule *and you still get ready on time*, you're going to be pretty disappointed with the number of makeup re-applications or hair touch-ups you'll need. Allow the day to begin to unfold before you truly sit down to start the process. I mean, I know you're excited, but if you are getting ready at 8am and your first look is not until 2pm, you are going to have a lot of downtime and makeup re-applications. While there is nothing wrong with extra time, everyone just gets antsy, and at times even wished they slept more. *So, don't rush your readiness.* Relatedly, it is best for the bride to be last for hair and makeup, that way her look is the freshest for photos.

Another tip I give all of my clients because of its importance is to note that your *invite time and start time of the ceremony should be 30 minutes apart.* This is because it will take people time to beat traffic, locate the venue, park their cars, say hi to a friend, and so many more variables. People tell me all the time how punctual their family is and while that may be true, many outside factors unfold on a wedding day (just like any other day) and keep it from being entirely predictable.

Following the ceremony is, of course, the long-awaited cocktail hour, which (as I mentioned before) is usually an hour. Although I previously discussed the benefits of taking family photos before the ceremony, I hold a different opinion at other times. If you know your family members always run late or you have a very large family, I suggest scheduling the family photos directly after the ceremony. This is because the whole family is there by that time: divorced parents, step-parents, half siblings, you get the point. If it makes it simpler, you can even give your family a heads-up about the pre-cocktail hour pics via email prior to the event. That way you're not doing any hunting, and the pictures are done quickly.

Next, *your reception times* will be partly built around food and beverage service, as dinner is generally a main component to the party. But the timeline will also include some key points such as (but not limited to) your grand entrance, first dance, parents' dances, toasts, cake-cutting, bouquet and garter tosses, and any other special things you want to have happen at your reception. Although it's impossible for me to know your personality or what you'd like to see happening at your reception, most couples' priorities include *a hearty party and dancing*. With that in mind, it is always good to make sure you have a few dance sets broken up throughout the reception.

As a videographer and an occasional wedding guest, it's often painful for me to watch the lack of energy at the reception when the schedule leaves the dancing for the very end. It forces guests to go from sitting during the ceremony, to drinking cocktails, to sitting some more amidst the reception highlights. By that point, your guests have been on their bottoms the majority of the time, and getting them onto the dance floor will likely prove to be a difficult task. That leads me to another piece of timeline advice: don't go long between dance sets. It'll keep the energy up longer, and no one will want to leave because they're engaged, too.

When I see people who were at my wedding, they are still talking about how much fun they had nearly a decade later. For me, my biggest wedding takeaway was all the amazing energy and endless fun our guests had. When people ask what I think made our wedding so different from others, I attribute it to the timeline (of course a couple who loves each other and truly is excited to get married helps, too). My wife and I knew we wanted a really fun event, and to make sure everyone had a blast was key. So, when writing our timeline, we did our grand entrance and went right into a short three-song, high energy dance set.

Picture our DJ announcing us in his booming voice. After bursting through the reception doors, we made our way into the room and *encouraged our family and friends to join us*. The music was blasting, and the dance floor was packed in an instant. No one was seated at that point; even the grandparents were doing a jig. And that vibe was *just what we wanted*.

From there, we requested everyone take a seat and we went into formalities (such as first dance, parents' dances, and toasts). A hint in regards to toasts is to always *try* to avoid planning them at the same time as salads or dinner. I only say this because most of the time the clink-clanking of the wait staff distracts your guests from the speaker. Of course, there's still the incessant utensil against the champagne glass noise, too. Thus, things cannot always be timed perfectly, I just like to offer perspective to ease the planning process.

After the formalities (which offer your guests a little dancing lull), I suggest a music set that starts a little softer. This is a great opportunity to include some slow, possibly more romantic dances. The audience always enjoys that, especially when it leads right into some more fun, upbeat tunes. Then once the grub is served and enjoyed, *party on.* The last most common practice to schedule is the cutting of the cake. I have found that some couples do not want to stop the party just to cut cake and feed each other. This is a personal preference and will really depend on how much dancing you want to have. Something to consider is that every time you stop the music, you run the risk of people not coming back on the dance floor. So, again, it all comes down to preference.

With all of that invaluable information said, here are two sample timelines to consider, one being with a first look (directly from my own wedding) and the other without.

With a First Look

12:30 PM - Bride getting ready (photo & video start with bride)

1:30 PM - Bride gets in dress

2:00 PM - Bride goes to venue

1:00 PM - Groom getting ready (photo & video assistants)

1:50 PM - Groom goes to venue

2:15 PM - First look and bridal party pictures

3:15 PM - Romantics (a photographer's term for extra couple shots))

4:15 PM - Family pictures

5:00 PM - Guest arrival

5:30/6:00 PM - Ceremony

6:00 PM - Cocktails

7:00 PM - Doors open for reception

7:20 PM - Grand entrance and mini dance set

7:40 PM - Moms will speak

7:45 PM - Salad served, wine and champagne poured

7:55 PM - Toasts (3)

8:10 PM - Main Course is served (for vendors, too)

8:40 PM - First dance, father-daughter dance & mother-son dance

8:55 PM - Dance set

9:30 PM - Cake cutting, bride and groom thank you, bouquet, garter

9:50 PM - Dancing all night!

Without a First Look

1:00 PM - Bride getting ready (photo & video start with bride)

2:00 PM - Bride to get in dress

2:30 PM - Bride goes to country club

2:15 PM - Groom getting ready (photo & video assistants)

3:05 PM - Groom goes to country club

3:30 PM - Bride, bridesmaids, and bride's family (if you choose to do this now, but many more photos needs to be taken with spouse added after)

4:15 PM - Groom, groomsmen and grooms family (if you choose to do this now, but many more photos needs to be taken with spouse added after)

5:00 PM - Guest arrival

5:30/6:00 PM - Ceremony

6:00 PM - Cocktails *and* family photos, bridal party, and romantics

7:00 PM - Doors open for reception

7:20 PM - Grand entrance and mini dance set

7:40 PM - Moms will speak

7:45 PM - Salad served; wine and champagne poured

7:55 PM - Toasts (3)

8:10 PM - Main Course is served (VENDORS EAT!)

8:40 PM - First dance, father-daughter dance & mother-son dance

8:55-9:25 PM - Dance set

9:30 PM - Cake cutting, bride and groom thank you, bouquet, garter

9:50 PM - Dancing all night!

Chapter 12

Crucial, No B.S. Tips That Don't Fit Anywhere Else

Advice for the wedding-planning process:

Planning a wedding might be something you've dreamed of for some time, or it might be a newer project. Either way, keep in mind **this day is about you and your spouse-to-be as a couple.** It's important to make sure both partners are involved as much as they want to be. As soon as you begin to discuss your wedding, it's generally a good idea to discuss what parts each of you want to be involved in or not involved in. Maybe your partner wants to go to the DJ meeting because music is important to them, or to the tasting because they love food. I've also seen some partners have *zero interest in planning* at all and give all creative freedom to their fiancee. **Any level of interest is okay,** and should be respected by the other person. It may require one of you being a bit more go with the flow, or both of you taking on different tasks to balance the workload; either way you work it out, just make sure both of you feel honored in the process, so no potential resentment lingers later. Again, communication is key to any relationship, not just a wedding, and this is an extra special time to use communication to your advantage so you can have a beautiful start to your new life.

In preparation for your big day, I would suggest **creating a simple wedding website** that will also connect your registry. The wedding website should be a tidy space for people to find information, possibly read about your relationship history, see engagement photos, view hotel room blocks, and find times and details for the big day. Invitations are misplaced all the time, so a website or landing page is a quick reference for guests to pop back to or bookmark. This is also the perfect spot to highlight your registry for everyone to view and order gifts.

In terms of your gift registry, I would truly take time to consider what you may want or need for your home. If you have most of what you need already, there is nothing wrong with putting a few extra things on your registry, as you can return them and get credit for it at a later time. Another logical option would be to start a honeymoon fund for your travels, as well as different activities and excursions. Quite honestly, people love adding to a honeymoon fund because they know it is for a once in a lifetime trip, filled with some of the first memories you will create as a married couple. If you have a house filled with goods and your honeymoon is taken care of, you can always add a cash fund for people to give to. Just consider that guests love knowing what you plan to buy with the fund. Is it for your home, or to launch a small business? Tell them!

Keep in mind though, I have found throughout my life that people would much rather give an item or activity than cash, and they tend to spend more if it's for something tangible. As an example, let's consider the holidays. If you ask for a gift that's around $100 a family member may be inclined to buy it for you, but if you simply ask for cash, they will typically gift you $50 or $75. Same thought process goes for wedding gifts and registries of all types.

Advice for the days preceding your wedding:

Congrats! You've hit the sweet spot, a.k.a. event time. I *highly* suggest that you **take off work and remove yourself from wedding planning 48-72 hours prior to your wedding.** Leave everything to your planner, maid of honor, or whoever you trust to make any decisions. Let this person or people know that you are relaxing and taking in the process. Unless there is some major issue, you are not to be bothered and you trust they will figure it out. You hired these vendors to make your day what you imagined and at this point they should do their job and not bother you with any small questions. Disconnect from planning involvement, get pampered, relax at the pool, go golfing, and just enjoy the last few days before the big day.

By the way, now is when I want to warn you about rehearsal dinners. Being one of the first times *everyone* gathers together, it can be pretty exciting to get your guests under one roof. Consequently, the drinks start flowing and before you know it, a few hours later the wedding day is here. As a videographer, the worst thing is arriving at a venue only to find a bride, groom, bridal party, or other guests doctoring a mean hangover. It definitely doesn't set the best stage for your day. People will be feeling sick, and most likely running very late. If it's bad enough, they'll be nursing themselves until late in the day, which always results in a lot of regrets you cannot rewind. So have fun, but try to **keep in mind what is happening** *the day after the rehearsal.*

Speaking of guests, when you are giving your final guest count to your venue (for food), you will likely be asked about vendor meals for vendors staying throughout the wedding day. A vendor meal is a discounted meal provided by the client for the vendors working their event. If vendor meals are purchased they're generally given to the wedding coordinator and their team, photographer(s), videographer(s), and DJ or band. Sometimes the meal is a small buffet for vendors set up in another room. Maybe it's a simple chicken dish. The meal can even be what the guests are eating; the venue or the clients generally give you the option to choose. Please know that your *vendors' meals are almost always heavily discounted.* I've had clients ask if I require a meal or if they need to purchase one for me. While I do not **require** this in my contract (though some vendors do), it is always nice to eat at a wedding. **It is even nicer to eat the same meal as the wedding guests.** When I got married, we gave our vendors the same options as the guests because they were with us all day. Since all of their hard work resulted in our dream wedding day, the least we could do to say we appreciated them was to give them a chance to sit for 15 minutes and eat a meal. So, when asked if you'll be hosting vendor meals, I always state an emphatic, "Yes!"

Another activity I support enthusiastically in the days prior to your wedding is self-care. As the event nears, you may feel a bit of increased pressure or stress. It is important you take some time to do things you enjoyed before the wedding planning process began, maybe even before you found your partner. Take care of yourself and reduce your stress levels before they climb even more. That way you'll enter your wedding weekend with a peaceful, excited approach.

Advice for the ceremony:

From a videographer's standpoint, I am always sure to suggest that you **have your wedding party sit down during the ceremony.** I know that sounds weird, but I suggest this because everyone has different plans of who they want to have stand with them at the altar. Sometimes it's requested that all the bridesmaids and groomsmen stand with the bride and groom. Other times everyone but the Maid and Man of Honor are seated. I've even had the horrific experience of watching a bridesmaid, who was locking her knees, faint at the altar. From my professional standpoint, there are so many people often crowding the altar that your photographer and videographer are blocked from getting certain shots. A great solution is one I came up with at my wedding (go figure).

We asked the bridal party to walk down the aisle, then the men seated themselves in the second row on my side, while the ladies did the same on my wife's side. The bridal party sat behind the immediate family, while the best man and maid of honor stood up at the altar with us. When the ceremony ended and we recessed, each pair met and still walked back down the aisle. This was nice because nobody was distracted by the bridal party during the ceremony, and we achieved near-perfection with our photo and video.

Advice for the cocktail hour & reception:

One of the most common, yet random, questions I receive in regards to receptions has to do with *photo booths*. While photo booths can be fun, I think there is a time and place for them for a few reasons. I know people love getting the pictures and sharing them online, and sometimes they can even serve as a party favor of sorts. I only caution *about time and location* of your photo booth.

1. I suggest having it during cocktail hour and if you are extending it into the reception, I would limit the time. This is because you do not want people in the booth taking pictures when your grand entrance is taking place; same goes for people making noise during toasts.

2. As for location, if you are continuing your photo booth hours into the reception, I would suggest not having the photo booth in a different room than the reception. This would be because it may draw your guests out of the room and this can hinder the party attendance. Again, it is all about personal preference, but just something to keep in mind.

Another common question I receive is, "Who should make speeches?"

To which I like to ask, "Have you been to a wedding in which you zoned out because every toast was an inside joke? How about people who did not prepare something and just rambled off random thoughts?" **In my humble opinion, the worst is the never-ending toasters.** I would give some serious thought to who should speak. While doing so, consider that I highly recommend only your maid or matron of honor and best man speak. Parents are also great at opening the night with some sort of welcome toast.

No matter who you choose, I highly suggest you **limit the number of toasts at your event.** An open mic is a *huge* *no-no* for many reasons, of which include timing, alcohol consumption, and having no control over who speaks. *The best time for others to speak is the rehearsal dinner.* Since this is usually dinner-and-mingle time, it is the perfect time for others to toast. You can even leave the floor open to anyone who might want to share well-wishes or stories.

When I got married we knew we only wanted a few to speak at the wedding, so we let our family and bridal party know that the rehearsal dinner was the perfect chance to toast us, if they wanted. Knowing how many people would speak, we hired a videographer for 2 hours so we could capture these toasts, which we have never regretted, because having those on video is absolutely priceless for us.

Advice for after the wedding:

Let's start somewhere near and dear to my heart. In terms of tipping vendors, there is no right or wrong. I think tipping in general is a nice gesture when you have received great service. But who do you tip? I've heard through the wedding grapevine that some customers don't find it necessary to tip a vendor if they *own* the company that's being hired. While I am the owner of a company, I suppose I can see why people say this. However, I feel tipping is always the kindest thing to do, no matter your vendor's role. It should be about the quality of service you are receiving. It should also be done at the end of the night, or when a particular service ends.

And what if the vendor did a bad job or was late? Then either give them something small or nothing, as you would probably do the same if you received the same service by a waiter at a restaurant. Ultimately though, tipping is truly at your discretion and should be handled vendor-to-vendor. I never expect a tip from any client, but whatever may be given is always beyond appreciated. I have received cash tips, various gifts, bottles of wine, gift cards, thank you cards, and many other items over the years. The thoughtfulness is what always stays with me when I receive a token of a couple's appreciation.

Also, be sure to write thank you notes. I know it seems like an outdated practice, but everyone appreciates them. I have known people to remember a thank you note they received as clearly as they remember the wedding they attended.

One last crucial no B.S. tip:

If you were to call me on the phone right now and say "Brian, I read your book and loved it. But what three things do you hope I learned from it?"

I would say 1) to hire a videographer, 2) plan a first look, and 3) start the reception with a small, upbeat dance set. Because that'll ensure your event is full of the happiest, most beautiful moments… captured on video.

Chapter 13

What to Expect & My Hope For Your Big Day

I have been at this whole wedding thing for a while. And in the process, I've seen some of the wedding world's craziest. Not only have I seen a bridesmaid faint (as I hinted at before), but I've also seen a bride collapse. She was just fine and came to within a few minutes, but the momentary swaying and hard fall is never easy to watch at a wedding (P.S. this is my chance to remind you all to eat a balanced breakfast that morning, drink plenty of fluids, and avoid locking your knees).

I recall one wedding where the power went out in the middle of a dance set. Small emergency lights at the edges of the room were triggered. Those, along with my video light, were more than enough to keep all the guests dancing and singing the song that had just stopped. A few minutes later, the power returned. Nobody cared, nobody worried, they just went with it. And what a moment it was to capture!

When I left a wedding one night, I noticed a little bag of chocolate hearts hanging from my rear view mirror. It was from the couple, and the valet had placed them in all of the cars during the event.

It said, "Thank you for being a part of our day. Love Always."

Even though this was towards the earlier part of my career, it has stayed with me. I thought it was just the perfect touch to end the day with.

I have been a part of almost every type of religious and cultural event known to exist. Some of the traditions I have seen over the years are beyond special to witness, and it's amazing to learn what they symbolize. Similarly, one of my favorite things to witness is a multi-cultural event. The unity of two people from very different backgrounds is powerful. This couple will bring both old cultural traditions and form new ones in their families. Witnessing them meld at their weddings is powerful, too; to see family, language, and love bring new depths to old worlds enriches my love for my job even more.

In less glamorous times, I once saw a few women tear flowers to shreds (and almost each other) amidst a bouquet toss. One time, a bride had to leave her reception after a nightmare toast or two. A wedding I once filmed had heavy security as means of keeping out a dangerous relative. I watched a bride traipse down an aisle right after her dog had pooped on it. I've seen newlyweds dancing on a table that was being lifted over the heads of wedding guests. There have been ice sculptures in the shape of the bride and groom, dove releases, food trucks, cigar rollers, money dances that covered the entire floor with cash, and place cards with hand-drawn caricatures of every guest. I have even seen an entire wedding (guests included) jump in the pool at the venue when the reception ended. I've seen celebrity after celebrity at some events, and hotel ballrooms re-carpeted for others. The list goes on and on.

With all of that said, I want you to think about what each of those weddings have in common. No matter how different, eccentric, dramatic, or heartwarming they might have been, they are all bits of a couple's *special day*.

And just that. One day. In fact, that whole book you just read... the one I spent months writing and years amassing knowledge for... it's all about *one day*. Hopefully the best day of your life, sure. But it's for one ceremony that lasts under an hour. And then it's one party, lasting *maybe* four hours. Five hours total, that you have spent infinite time and energy planning.

And I will say this: the event itself goes by fast. Virtually in the blink of an eye, just as the rest of life does. Thus, it is your duty as the couple getting hitched to try to enjoy each step of the wedding process and the day. You will never spend as much time, energy, or money on a single day ever again. *Enjoying it is a must.*

I say this because I hear so many brides or grooms wish it all away with a simple, "Can't it just all be over already?"

But afterwards they're all left feeling like they've missed things that were muddled by their worries or stress. It's so easy to get lost in these things, these small details or opinions.

At which point I like to remind my couples (and I repeat):

It's all about one day, hopefully the best day of your life. But it's for one ceremony that lasts about an hour. And then it's one party, lasting *maybe* four hours. Sure, it's the introduction to your love story, or maybe you're already a few chapters in. Either way, it is not the end all be all. It does not dictate the rest of your relationship. Nothing about your wedding should ultimately be life-altering. It may represent your love right now, but your love will grow so much more over the years. And how many times have you seen those awful memes with horrific bridesmaids dresses and tuxes? I mean, *people thought those outfits were good ideas at one point.*

What I'm getting at is that the most important thing about your wedding remains to be what I said from the get-go: **you and your partner.** Not the tiny details of your centerpieces, or the folding of your invitation envelopes. While we are on this, please know you may walk into your wedding and see a certain table out of place, perhaps a mistake with your flowers or even the wrong song being played at a specific time. Just know, *it's all good. Nobody knows but you.* Roll with it because there isn't much more you can do about it once things are going. You can talk to your planner if need be, or just laugh it off and keep having fun. Remember, the point of this wedding is to marry your person, your best friend, the love of your life.

I wish you a wonderful rehearsal dinner, which is always a great warm-up to the big day. It is also an intimate gathering of your closest friends and family. It should fill you with love and excitement before you tie the knot. Try to get some sleep despite any jitters you may feel (which are totally normal). Just remember, you are marrying this person for a reason, don't let the "wedding" cloud that.

And really try to take a moment on your big day with your spouse to **just look around and take it all in.** Look at the beauty, detail, and hard work that has gone into this event. Look at all these people who stopped their lives to be with you on this most special day.

I wish you and your spouse the most amazing wedding, and I truly hope in my heart that this book has helped you feel as if you are ready to tackle your planning. In the end it will all work out and be beautiful, which is exactly what you deserve.

NOTES

_____

_____

_____

_____

_____

_____

_____

_____

_____

_____

_____

_____

Made in the USA
Las Vegas, NV
21 September 2021

30781906R30066